Live a new life

Live a new life

David Watson

Inter-Varsity Press

INTER-VARSITY PRESS

Universities and Colleges Christian Fellowship
39 Bedford Square, London WC1B 3EY

© INTER-VARSITY PRESS, LONDON

First edition November 1975

ISBN 0 85110 388 X

Printed in Great Britain by
Richard Clay (The Chaucer Press), Ltd.,
Bungay, Suffolk

Contents

Acknowledgments

The author is very grateful to Mary Pratt for her patient typing of the manuscript, and to Andrew Cornes for his helpful suggestions on reading the original draft.

Preface

Dear David,

I'm just dropping this note to say that I feel I have found Christ. The change has been gradual over the past four weeks or so, but my experiences over this weekend have finally clinched it.

Of course 'Rome wasn't built in a day' and I do not expect suddenly and completely to alter my life-style over-night, but some inward change has definitely taken place.

I should be grateful if you could tell me where I should go from here.

Yours very sincerely,
Graham

This is an extract from one of numerous letters I have been privileged to receive. Graham, in fact, was a university student at the time; and he, together with many others who have come to a personal commitment to Christ, was anxious to go ahead in the Christian faith.

This book is written to help those who, like Graham, really want the best—God's best—for their life.

1 'I know where I'm going'

Bob, a young man in his twenties, had become a Christian quite recently. At an evening service in my church I asked him to tell the congregation something of his story, and in particular what had brought him to Christ. He replied by saying that a few months ago he was in a state of confusion concerning the direction of his life. On the surface it was not apparent; indeed he was showing considerable promise as a pilot in the Royal Air Force. But inwardly he was asking basic questions about the meaning and purpose of life.

If there is one word which sums up today's situation more than any other, it is this word *confusion*. When there is enough nuclear explosive stockpiled for mankind to destroy itself 50,000 times over, and when the population of the world is expected to double in twenty-five years and already thirty million die each year because they are too hungry to live, we can understand why there is such confusion. Indeed there seem to be no answers to such problems as violence, strife, strikes, mental illness, economic crises, and to the confusion which exists at every level from personal to international.

Moreover, this bewilderment considerably increases the sense of futility which so many feel today. Where can we find a clear sense of direction? Is there any purpose to life at all? Most contemporary thinkers seem almost haunted by the problem of meaningless existence. Why did Carl Jung say that 'the central neurosis of our time is emptiness'? Why is there this constant confusion—not always outwardly obvious, but often to be found in more reflective moments?

The reason is this: life has no ultimate meaning apart from God. Indeed, God has given each of us a large spiritual appetite which cannot be satisfied by anything less than himself. Therefore Jesus came as 'the bread of life' to satisfy our hunger,[1] and as the 'light of the world' to give us direction and purpose.[2]

In one of his most famous invitations Jesus once said this: 'Come to me, all who labour and are heavy laden, and I will give you rest. Take my yoke upon you, and learn from me; for I am gentle and lowly in heart, and you will find rest for your souls. For my yoke is easy, and my burden is light.'[3] I want to look more closely at that invitation, and ask five questions about it.

1. Who can come? Answer, in the words of Jesus: 'All who labour and are heavy laden.' This is, therefore, a selective invitation; it is not for everyone. It is for those who are tired of the pressures and problems in their lives. Until I am personally conscious of my

[1] John 6:35   [2] John 8:12
[3] Matthew 11:28-30

need, therefore, and am willing to admit it, Christ has nothing for me.

My particular problem might not be confusion or meaninglessness; it might be something quite different. But most of our problems, ultimately, are symptoms of a much more deep-rooted problem which is common to every person. Paul once expressed it like this: 'There is no distinction; since all have sinned and fall short of the glory of God.'[4] We have all gone our own way and have broken God's laws. We all need the help and forgiveness of Jesus Christ. It is this inescapable fact of sin which blinds our spiritual understanding, makes God seem unreal, and robs life of its true meaning.

Once we realize this and humbly admit it, Christ's invitation is intensely relevant: 'Come to me, all who labour and are heavy laden.'

2. *Why should I come?* In practice many people do not have strong feelings about their need of God. Feelings anyway are frequently misleading. Rather we should humbly accept the objective diagnosis of our true condition. Since God is God, what he has to say about our need is of the utmost importance. His authority is supreme. Indeed, Christ frequently made it unmistakably clear that, as King of kings and Lord of lords, he alone has the right to speak on all the greatest issues of life and death. His invitation, therefore, like all 'royal' invitations, is a command. The question of whether or not we happen to *feel* a need is comparatively unimportant. In the physical realm there is a condition called euphoria, when someone may feel

[4] Romans 3:22, 23

surprisingly well but in fact is very sick. There can also be a spiritual euphoria. The first step towards knowledge of God lies, therefore, in a humble acceptance of his authority over our lives. When Jesus tells us to 'repent, and believe in the gospel',[5] this is not good advice to those who happen to be conscious of some need. It is a command.

In the New Testament the alternative before us is clearly expressed several times: either we believe in Christ, *or we disobey him*. Since he is Lord of all, to whom one day every person must submit, this must be so. John wrote: 'Whoever believes in the Son has eternal life; whoever disobeys the Son will never have life, but God's wrath will remain on him for ever.'[6] And Paul once said that God's judgment would one day come on those 'who do not know God and ... who do not *obey* the Good News about our Lord Jesus'.[7]

3. What happens if I come? Answer: 'I will give you rest.... You will find rest for your souls.' In our restless society there are few promises more meaningful.

Travel agencies offer rest only when we 'get away from it all'. Entertainment offers escape from our true situation. The real and important world, however, is to begin with the world inside, and not the world outside. I may change my outside world completely— my friends, my work, my home. But if I have no peace and rest inside, in my heart, the change alters very little. On the other hand, if my mind and heart are at rest, I have something of immeasurable value which nothing can remove.

[5] Mark 1:15   [6] John 3:36 (TEV)
[7] 2 Thessalonians 1:8 (TEV)

This is exactly what Jesus offers through his death for our sins. On the cross he took our place and bore our guilt and punishment. At first Simon Peter could not understand why Jesus had to die; but later he put it like this: 'Christ died for our sins once and for all. He, the just, suffered for the unjust, to bring us to God.'[8] What does this mean? The essence of sin is that we go our way, not God's, and therefore inevitably we find ourselves separated from him. That is why God is unreal in our experience. Think of this in terms of two banks on either side of a river. By going our own way, and not God's, we are on one bank and God on the other. Now, if traffic is to flow from one side to the other, we need a bridge which, by definition, touches both sides. In the history of the world there has only been one bridge which is both God and man, and that is Jesus Christ. Moreover, he could effectively become that bridge for us only by taking upon himself the problem which caused the separation in the first place, namely our sin. That is why Peter said, 'Christ also died for our sins ... to bring us to God.' Further, it is through the cross that we can have peace with God and the peace *of* God in our hearts. The barrier of sin was dealt with once and for all when Jesus died, and we receive the benefits of his death when we receive him into our lives.

4. *On what conditions do I come?* Answer, in the words of Jesus: 'Take my yoke upon you, and learn from me.' Here Jesus is using a farming picture in which two animals (usually oxen) were yoked together for the purpose of some task, such as ploughing a field.

[8] 1 Peter 3:18 (NEB)

The yoke would consist of a wooden frame which held the two animals together and kept them moving in the same direction. If, then, we are to come to Jesus, we must be willing, from now onwards, to go with him.

This is essential in all true conversions. Conversion involves a change of direction: instead of going my own way and doing my own thing, I turn round and start going with Jesus Christ. But, unless I am willing to let him guide and direct my life as he wants, I cannot know the peace and rest that he offers.

The reason is simple. It is Jesus who gives me peace; it is Jesus who gives me rest—not 'religion', nor 'trying hard'. Only Jesus can do that. If I am to know his rest in my heart and his direction in my life, therefore, I must come to him and go with him. He must have control and authority in my life. 'Take my yoke upon you, and learn from me.' And if that seems too costly, remember that his yoke is easy and his burden light. He will give us a degree of freedom that we can find nowhere else, a freedom to live the best possible life that God has planned for us.

5. *How do I come?* Answer: You come just as you are! Our life may be highly successful, or in a mess; God may seem terribly remote, or very near; we may have been searching for him for years, or only just started thinking about him; we may feel ashamed, confused, afraid, uncertain. It all makes not the slightest difference at all. If I humbly admit my need of Christ and of his forgiveness, I come to him just as I am, with all my sins and failings and doubts and fears, and I hand the whole lot over to him.

In one well-known promise, the risen Christ, standing outside the house of our life, says, 'Behold, I stand at the door and knock; if any one hears my voice and opens the door, I will come in.'[9] He longs to enter our lives, to bring his forgiveness and love and to make God real in our lives. If he comes, he will stay. Only then can we know the peace and rest which he alone can bring.

The essential factor in all this is faith. Faith is not some complicated religious term; it simply means *taking someone at their word*. Here we are to trust the word of Christ; and as soon as we believe his promise and ask him to enter our life, we begin at that moment a new, personal, and lasting relationship with him.

Is this what you have done? If you are not quite sure, it would be helpful and sensible to become sure by 'inking over' what you may have already done in pencil. The New Testament Christians were quite convinced about their experience of the risen Christ, and it was this deep assurance which gave them spiritual vitality and a clear sense of direction. They knew where they were going.

If you lack the assurance of a personal relationship with God through Jesus Christ, pray this prayer quietly on your own. Don't be in a hurry: take time, and be still in God's presence before you pray.

Lord Jesus Christ,
I admit that I have sinned and gone my own way.
I need your forgiveness.
Thank you for your love, especially in dying on the
    cross to take away my sin.

[9] Revelation 3:20

15

I am willing for you to lead and direct my life.
And now I come to you, Lord Jesus.
I ask you to be my Saviour and Friend and Lord for
ever.
Amen.

Have you prayed that, and really meant it—or perhaps a similar prayer some time ago? If so, you must take Christ at his word and believe that he *has now* entered your life in the person of his Spirit. Feelings at this stage are unimportant. Some people experience a tremendous quality of peace; others have no feelings whatsoever. It makes no difference. It is his promise that is all important. He never breaks his word.

2 New birth

'When someone becomes a Christian', wrote Paul, 'he becomes a brand new person inside. He is not the same any more. A new life has begun!'[1] In fact Paul was so excited about this that he dropped the main verb, and the original Greek reads like a newspaper headline: 'If anyone is in Christ—NEW CREATION!' Here is really something to shout about!

Some feel this newness immediately.

'It's like starting all over again.'
'I never realized what a difference it would make.'
'I was a new person altogether.'
'I feel like a complete beginner with a new outlook.'
'I have just woken up to life.'
'I felt a completely different person.'
'My whole world has changed.'

These are some of the expressions used in letters I have received. For others the experience of this new-

[1] 2 Corinthians 5:17 (Living Bible)

ness is much more gradual, though none the less real. Never worry if your experience is not quite the same as someone else's. God deals with each of us as individuals, and different personalities are bound to react in different ways. What then happens when a person commits his life whole-heartedly to Christ?

The spiritual change following a true conversion should ultimately be so revolutionary that the New Testament rightly describes it as a *new birth*. Indeed Jesus made it painfully clear to the religious leader, Nicodemus, that until someone is 'born again' he can neither see nor enter the kingdom of God: spiritually he is blind and dead to it without this rebirth. 'You must be born again,' said Jesus.[2]

But how can I know that I am born again? If I rest on my feelings as a Christian I am in for a rough time. Feelings are notoriously deceptive; they are a hopeless barometer for spiritual reality and depend on such mundane matters as food and sleep and physical condition. Therefore how can I *know* that I am born again?

John tackles this question in his first Letter, which was written to Christians to assure them of their relationship with God. The Letter is peppered with the words 'we know', and it was written expressly 'that you may know that you have eternal life'.[3]

Think for a moment of sitting on a three-legged stool. If all three legs are correctly in place, your position is quite stable; if one leg is short, or even missing altogether, you will wobble; if two legs are absent, you will be most insecure; if all legs are removed—crash! The three 'legs' of Christian assurance are these: The

[2] John 3:3–8   [3] 1 John 5:13

18

Word of God, the work of Christ, the witness of the Spirit.

1. The Word of God, as seen primarily and objectively in the Scriptures. 'He who has the Son has life,' wrote John;[4] and therefore, when you trust Christ's word and act upon it by asking him into your life, you can know that he has come according to his promise and that you now have eternal life. Peter said much the same: 'Through the living and eternal word of God you have been born again.'[5] And Jesus taught that the wise person 'hears these words of mine and acts upon them'. The house of his life would stand firmly on the rock (of Christ and his word), even in the midst of storm and tempest.[6]

When Jesus himself was being buffeted by doubt, shortly after his Father had said to him 'You are my beloved Son', he countered Satan with the Word of God. Three times he said 'It is written ...', quoting from the Scriptures.[7] It was in this way that he stood firm on the rock. Rely on subjective experiences and you will be up and down like a yo-yo; but depend on the objective facts of God's promises, and you have a basic stability to your faith that nothing can finally shake. 'Scripture cannot be broken,' said Jesus. Here are a few well-tried promises for you to remember and claim.

'I give them eternal life, and they shall never perish, and no one shall snatch them out of my hand.'

[4] 1 John 5:12
[6] Matthew 7:24–27 (NEB)
[5] 1 Peter 1:23 (TEV)
[7] Matthew 4:1–11

'I will never fail you nor forsake you.'

'I am with you always, to the close of the age.'

'Him who comes to me I will not cast out.'[8]

In your own reading of the Bible you will find it valuable to add to these promises, and to learn them, perhaps writing them down in a notebook. Many find this of considerable help, especially in the early days.

2. *The work of Christ* The next important factor in your assurance is the work of Christ, in particular his finished work when he died on the cross 'once for all' to take away our sins. Indeed John assures his readers, 'The blood of Jesus ... cleanses us from *all* sin.... (Therefore) if we confess our sins, he is faithful and just, and will forgive our sins and cleanse us from *all* unrighteousness.'[9] Notice the repetition of that crucial word 'all'. Christ's death is sufficient for us; the sacrifice for sins is complete. What is necessary for complete forgiveness for all sin has once for all been finished.[1] The freedom and joy of those first Christians stemmed in large part from the glorious assurance that, although they were manifestly sinful in the eyes of a holy God, they had now been absolutely forgiven, cleansed, released and reconciled to God. There was no barrier between them and God any more. They were sons of God, and had immediate access into his presence at any time 'by the blood of Jesus'.

Is this presumptuous? No more so than the attitude of my two children who know that they can come to me at any time and look up into my face and say

[8] John 10:28; Hebrews 13:5; Matthew 28:20; John 6:37
[9] 1 John 1:7, 9
[1] See Hebrews 9:26–28; 10:10–22; 1 Peter 3:18; *etc.*

'Daddy!' Indeed, something would be fundamentally wrong if they became unsure of their relationship with me. This is the confidence that you and I are meant to have, based not on our own merits but on the finished work of Christ on the cross. 'It is finished' was his own cry shortly before he died. This word (*tetelestai* in the Greek) has rightly been called 'the greatest single word ever uttered'. This is the one sure basis of a right relationship with God.

What happens, then, when I sin? Has my relationship with God been broken? Do I have to start all over again? The answer is emphatically No! My relationship with God is temporarily spoilt when I sin, but certainly not broken. When I am selfish or thoughtless at home, I may temporarily spoil my relationship with my wife, but I don't have to get married all over again! Instead I have to learn to say sorry and so restore the damage caused. So it is with God. Confess your sin, say sorry, turn away from what is wrong, and trust in his complete and absolute forgiveness, based always on what Jesus has accomplished for us on the cross.

3. *The witness of the Spirit* is the third stabilizing factor. Spiritual re-birth is entirely the work of the Spirit of God. A person turns from his sin to Christ (= conversion), but the Holy Spirit causes the new birth (= regeneration). Every true Christian has therefore the Spirit of Christ living with him. Indeed, 'anyone who does not have the Spirit of Christ does not belong to him'.[2]

But, if the Spirit of God is really present in a per-

[2] Romans 8:9

son's life, there must be some evidence of this. In the next chapter we shall look briefly at the 'tests of life' that John enumerates in his first Letter, but for the moment we should look at a statement made by Paul: 'When we cry "Abba! Father!" it is the Spirit himself bearing witness with our spirit that we are children of God.'[3] 'Abba' is the Aramaic equivalent of 'Dadda'—the natural, spontaneous cry of a young child to his father. Together, therefore, with the objective truths of Scripture and the historical facts of the cross, the Spirit gives us an inward, subjective assurance about our relationship with God, a deep personal conviction that I am his child and he is my Father. This is more than an intellectual appreciation of the integrity of the gospel; it is a profound, personal assurance of the father–child relationship. It is the Spirit speaking to our *spirit* (our innermost being), and not primarily to our mind, of the reality of this relationship.

Now this 'witness of the Spirit' is of considerable practical importance. Paul goes on at once (in this passage in Romans 8) to speak of the problems of suffering which await us in this world; but even suffering can be transformed when there is the conviction that 'in everything God works for good', that 'we are more than conquerors through him who loved us', and that absolutely nothing 'will be able to separate us from the love of God'.[4] This is the confidence of every child of God who, by the Spirit, can cry 'Abba! Father!'

Such a confidence comes to different Christians at different times and in different ways. Some have an almost immediate deep awareness of their new relation-

[3] Romans 8:15, 16; *cf.* Galatians 4:6   [4] Romans 8:28–39

22

ship with God. For others this awareness grows over a period of time as they grasp more fully the implications of their commitment to Christ. Others may discover a time when they are consciously filled with the Holy Spirit and they have a fresh and joyful experience of the love of their heavenly Father. The precise way in which God's Spirit 'speaks to us deep in our hearts, and tells us that we really are God's children'[5] will vary. No doubt God will assure us of this relationship on many occasions. But certainly he wants us to know, in a profound and personal way, that we belong to him and that nothing can alter his love for us.

Further, this spiritual new birth is so radical that Jesus gave a special individual sign for all those who had come to follow him: the sign of *water baptism*. Although Christians hold different views about the correct mode of baptism (immersion or sprinkling) and the valid age for baptism (adult or infant), baptism is unquestionably an outward sign depicting the blessings of the gospel. In particular it signifies union with Christ, cleansing from sin and the gift of the Holy Spirit, although, of course, the reality of what it signifies comes, not with the sign, but in answer to faith. Just as a wedding ring is an important sign of marriage, but is not the same as the solemn act of faith ('I will') or the subsequent relationship; so baptism is a meaningful sign of God's blessing in Christ, but is not the same as personal faith in Christ or the continuing relationship. All true disciples of Christ, however, should be baptized in the name of the Father, Son and Holy Spirit; and you may need to see a Christian minister or pastor about this.

[5] Romans 8:16 (Living Bible)

3 Signs of life

Clearly a genuine new birth (a single event) will be followed by a growing new life (a continuous process). Indeed, any claims for a new birth would at once become invalid unless the marks of the new life were increasingly in evidence. If someone says to me in winter, 'That is an apple tree!' I shall naturally expect to see blossom in spring and fruit in the summer. Otherwise I may investigate further!

John, in his first Letter, spells out some of the evidences of the new life that should become increasingly apparent in a true child of God. He was writing to Christians who, occasionally at least, had considerable doubts about their relationship with God and their actual spiritual condition. They had been confused by false teachers who were claiming to be sinless and yet led selfish and immoral lives. What, then, should they believe, and how should they behave? John gives at least eight signs of a healthy spiritual life.

1. A new family 'That which we have seen and heard

we proclaim also to you, so that you may have fellowship with us; and our fellowship is with the Father and with his Son Jesus Christ.... If we walk in the light, as he is in the light, we have fellowship with one another.'[1] That is one of the first signs that we really belong to God: we realize that we belong to other Christians as well. We have entered a new family, and new relationships are formed which may cut right across the man-made barriers of colour, class, education, age, or sex. We discover, at least in some measure, that 'we are all one in Christ Jesus'. Indeed, the church, as the family of God, ought to be a community of love, with its members as committed to one another as they are to Christ.

2. *A new obedience* 'By this we may be sure that we know him, if we keep his commandments.... You may be sure that every one who does right is born of him.'[2] By nature we are all the 'sons of disobedience'[3] in that we all do what we want, not what God wants. But a new desire to obey and please God is a good sign of spiritual life. We may sometimes disobey, of course, but basically the direction of our lives will be turned from self to God.

3. *A new love for God* 'Do not love the world or the things in the world. If any one loves the world, love for the Father is not in him.... And the world passes away, and the lust of it; but he who does the will of God abides for ever.'[4] Here the 'world' refers to anything which does not come under the lordship of

[1] 1 John 1:3, 7   [2] 1 John 2:3, 29
[3] Ephesians 2:2   [4] 1 John 2:15–17

Christ: John describes it as 'the lust of the flesh and the lust of the eyes and the pride of life'. Instead of these worldly attitudes there should be steadily developing within us a new love for God, and a new desire for his truth and his ways.

4. *A new hatred for sin* 'Whoever is a child of God does not continue to sin, because God's very nature is in him.'[5] Of course there will be frequent lapses when our self-life dominates once again, but it is a bad sign if we go on deliberately and habitually committing sin. If 'God is his Father, he is not able to continue to sin', says John; we should experience an increasing dislike, even hatred, for what we know is offensive to our Father in heaven.

5. *A new love for other Christians* 'We know that we have passed out of death into life, because we love the brethren. He who does not love remains in death.'[6] There should develop a new affinity for those who have now become our brothers and sisters in Christ. Not that we should think of this love simply in terms of a warm feeling. John goes on to explain that, with the love of Jesus in our hearts, 'we ought to lay down our lives for the brethren', and certainly our goods ought to be shared with those in need. And of course this new love will spill over to others who are not Christians, changing our attitude and approach towards everyone, regardless of personal likes and dislikes.

6. *A new peace* 'If our hearts (or consciences) do not

[5] 1 John 3:9 (TEV)   [6] 1 John 3:14

26

condemn us, we have confidence before God."[7] This may vary according to the understanding of forgiveness that a person may have. But many new Christians speak joyfully of 'a great weight off my shoulders' or 'peace of mind'. Often there is a sense of relief. King David, after the assurance of God's forgiveness following a serious moral relapse, once wrote this: 'What happiness for those whose guilt has been forgiven! What joys when sins are covered over! What relief for those who have confessed their sins and God has cleared their record.'[8]

7. *A new enemy* Several times John talks about 'the evil one',[9] 'the antichrist',[1] 'the liar',[2] 'the devil',[3] and the 'spirit of error'.[4] 'We know that we are of God,' he writes, 'and the whole world is in the power of the evil one.' When you become a Christian, therefore, you discover a new friend in Jesus and a new enemy in the devil. When you were 'in the power of the evil one' then, as a child in the arms of its mother, you may not have been greatly troubled by this enemy of God. But once you come into God's hands, then you will become aware of the reality of the evil one, perhaps as never before. You may be tempted more strongly than ever to say or do what you know is wrong. You may be tempted to doubt, to deny God, to fall out with your Christian friends, and you may feel the full force of sin and evil in your own life, as well as in the world. Some people get worried that this should be so. Surely something has gone wrong! No! You are merely ex-

[7] 1 John 3:21   [8] Psalm 32:1, 2 (Living Bible)
[9] 1 John 2:13, 14; 3:12; 5:18, 19   [1] 1 John 2:18, 22; 4:3
[2] 1 John 2:22   [3] 1 John 3:8, 10
[4] 1 John 4:6

periencing what every other Christian has experienced. Indeed, Christ himself had a tremendous battle with the devil just after his baptism, at the very start of his ministry. The time to get worried is when the devil leaves you alone because your Christian life is no longer a threat to him.[5]

8. *A new power over evil* 'Whatever is born of God overcomes the world.'[6] There will, of course, continue to be a struggle. Paul wrote vividly of the tug-o'-war between the flesh (our self-life with all its numerous and ugly manifestations) and the Spirit.[7] But God has not left us to battle away in our own strength. In one sense, the victory has already been won for us when Christ died on the cross. There Christ not only died *for us*, taking away the guilt of our sin, but also we died *with him*, breaking the power of our sin. Thus by virtue of our union with Christ we are dead to that old world of sin; we 'have crucified the flesh with its passions and desires'. We have instead been raised to a new realm, the kingdom of God, where Christ reigns and where we must learn to live and walk by the Spirit. Even though at times we may feel very much alive to the old world, if we claim by faith our new position and authority in Christ we shall find increasingly victory over the power of sin. As John rightly says, 'This is the victory that overcomes the world, our faith. Who is it that overcomes the world but he who believes that Jesus is the Son of God?'[8]

[5] See *The Screwtape Letters* by C. S. Lewis (Fontana) for a classic exposé of the devil's wiles.   [6] 1 John 5:4

[7] See Galatians 5:16–26; *cf.* Romans 6:1–14

[8] 1 John 5:4, 5. I have tried to explain this more fully in chapter 2 of my book *God's Freedom Fighters* (Movement Books).

28

4 Knowing God

You have started! You have committed your life to Christ; and, as we saw in our last two chapters, you have a new birth and the beginnings of a new life.

The most obvious questions at this stage, and ones which I am frequently asked, are these: What now? Where do I go from here? How can I keep it up?

Think of your new life in Christ in terms of relationships, which, after all, are the basis of all life. Those who are constantly seeking for special mystical experiences may soon be shipwrecked on the rocks of confusion, doubt or disillusionment, even though there are very real and rich experiences to be found in Christ. But the essence of it all can be seen in three sets of relationships. In this chapter we shall look at the first of these, *my relationship with God.*

As with all relationships the most important factor is good, open and honest communication. If we want any friendship to develop we must spend time with our friend, listen as well as speak, trust and act on what has been shared. A true friendship requires a mutual and constantly deepening commitment of one to the other. So it is with God.

To begin with we must *listen* to him. God, being a living God, can speak to us in a whole variety of ways: through creation, through other people (especially other Christians), through our situation, sometimes through suffering or disappointment or hardship, often directly to our conscience. But supremely he speaks to us through his written word in the Bible. It is through the 'living and abiding word of God' that we receive new birth,[1] and therefore it is through the same Word that we must sustain and nourish our new life: 'Like newborn babes, long for the pure spiritual milk (= the Word of God; see context), that by it you may grow up to salvation (= full spiritual life and strength); for you have tasted the kindness of the Lord.'[2] Often people tell me that they pray; but, if anything, prayerful Bible study is even more important. We must listen to God and feed upon his Word if we are to grow strong spiritually.

For most people a regular system of Bible reading is the most helpful way of receiving good, healthy spiritual food. The Scripture Union, for example, provides a well-tried system that has helped Christians all over the world. Introductory notes on Mark's Gospel (called *Way In*) are available and last for a month, followed by regular notes aiming to cover virtually the whole Bible over a period of time.[3] Start anyway with 'milk' rather than 'solid meat'; you will find that one of the Gospels is an excellent place to

[1] 1 Peter 1:23–25
[2] 1 Peter 2:2, 3
[3] Notes available from the Scripture Union, 47 Marylebone Lane, London W1M 6AX. Send for details.

30

begin. But do not rely *too* much on the teaching of the notes. Remember that you are dealing with spiritual truth, and the Bible therefore needs the illumination of the Holy Spirit before it means anything very much or becomes 'living and active' in our lives. Therefore always come prayerfully, asking God specifically to help you understand what you are reading.

Different versions of the Bible will be helpful for different people and for different purposes. For an accurate translation from the original text, and good for study, it is hard to better the Revised Standard Version (RSV), and this is much easier to read than the Authorized Version (AV), even though it loses some of the poetry of that much older translation. Even simpler, and one which is extremely readable, is Today's English Version (TEV); and at times, for a thoroughly fresh look at a passage, a paraphrase such as Kenneth Taylor's Living Bible or J. B. Phillips' translation is very helpful. Others may prefer the New English Bible or the Jerusalem Bible or one of the many other translations that are available today. To begin with, a good modern translation (such as the RSV or TEV) and a lively paraphrase (such as the Living Bible) might be a good combination. Ask an older Christian friend before you spend your money, as the variety of translations, sizes and prices can be thoroughly confusing!

Careful and prayerful Bible study can be immensely enriching. Moreover, since the message of the Bible is God's truth, he requires that we act on what we read. The more we obey him, the more we shall understand the significance of what he says to us.[4] God never

[4] See John 7:17

reveals himself to those who are merely curious, but to those who mean business and who genuinely want the best. Therefore Peter, when telling his readers to 'long for the pure spiritual milk', also told them to 'put away all malice and all guile and insincerity and envy and all slander'.[5] Unconfessed and unresolved sin will act like poison in our system and will spoil our appetite for God's Word. As a Christian once wrote in the flyleaf of his Bible, 'Either the Bible will keep you from sin, or sin will keep you from the Bible.'

Read a few verses at a time, and then try to digest what you have read. What does the passage or phrase mean? What did it mean for New Testament Christians? What does it mean for me, for us, today? This personal and devotional Bible study is like eating fish: some verses will be like the bones and stick in your mouth. Well, leave them on one side. They no doubt have a vital place, but not for you at the moment. Feed on the parts that you can digest and that strengthen your faith. Above all, come looking for Jesus Christ.

Having listened to God we must then *speak* to him in prayer. Most people find Bible reading helpful before prayer, because it is much easier speaking to God once he has spoken to you. Has he taught you, encouraged you, rebuked you, warned you, humbled you, strengthened you through his Word? Well then, turn that into prayer. 'Pray in' those thoughts until they take root, not only in your mind, but in your heart and life. Then use those same thoughts as the basis of your prayer for others. You may find it helpful to make a list of persons and needs that you want to remember in prayer. As you cannot pray for every-

[5] 1 Peter 2:1

thing every day, work out a simple prayer diary, and pray for different people and needs each day of the week.

Here a balance is very important. It is possible to develop such a fixed system of prayer lists that prayer becomes mechanical and increasing drudgery, until perhaps you give up altogether. It has all become quite meaningless to you in terms of real communication with the living God. But if you have no system at all, wishing to be more spontaneous and Spirit-led, this can so easily become carelessness and laziness. The balance is a delicate one, and lies somewhere in between. All of us need some real discipline before we can discover the immense power of prayer. At the same time, within this discipline we need to discover a freedom to pray as the Spirit leads us. Here again God promises to help us: 'The Spirit helps us in our weakness; for we do not know how to pray as we ought, but the Spirit himself intercedes for us with sighs too deep for words'—or 'in groans that words cannot express.'[6] Therefore if we acknowledge our weakness in prayer and pray specifically for the help of the Holy Spirit, we shall find an increasing longing to pray according to the will of God.

There is, of course, a great variety in prayer and we must not always be asking God for things. Some people find the word ACTS a simple mnemonic for the most basic forms of prayer.

Adoration Worship is the primary task of the Christian; it is even more important than witness. 'Come to (Jesus),' writes Peter, '... and ... offer

[6] Romans 8:26

33

spiritual sacrifices acceptable to God through Jesus Christ.[7] The New Testament speaks of three specific sacrifices 'acceptable to God', as we worship him for his supreme sacrifice of his Son. To understand these three sacrifices will help to give meaning to our adoration in prayer. First, there is the 'sacrifice of *praise* to God, that is, the fruit of lips that acknowledge his name'.[8] It is good, therefore, to begin prayer by quietly reflecting on the presence of God, and then praising him for his nature and his goodness towards us. You may find that some of the psalms are particularly helpful, or else hymns or spiritual songs. Time spent worshipping God with a sacrifice of praise will be time when our relationship with him is considerably enriched.

Secondly, there is the sacrifice of *possessions*: 'Share what you have, for such sacrifices are pleasing to God.'[9] Worship should never be allowed to degenerate into a super-spirituality. The Old Testament prophets constantly had to remind God's people that their religious life, expressed in praying and fasting, was not sufficient. No! God wanted them to share their bread with the hungry and bring the homeless poor into their house.[1] Real worship will include practical and costly sacrifice.

Thirdly, there is the sacrifice of our *persons*: 'Present your bodies as a living sacrifice, holy and acceptable to God, which is your spiritual worship.'[2] And Paul goes on to spell out what this involves. It means not being 'conformed to this world'; it means using every God-given gift to serve and build up other Christians; it means loving, giving, sharing, forgiving,

[7] 1 Peter 2:4, 5   [8] Hebrews 13:15   [9] Hebrews 13:16
[1] See Isaiah 58   [2] Romans 12:1

34

harmonious relationships. Therefore when we rightly start with worship and adoration we must remember that Christian love is never 'in word or speech' only, but also 'in deed and in truth'.[3] We are not to offer God that which costs us nothing.

Confession The commonest hindrance to prayer is unconfessed sin: 'If I had cherished iniquity in my heart, the Lord would not have listened.'[4] Further, confession needs to be specific. It is one thing to acknowledge, in formal Prayer Book language, that we are 'miserable offenders'; it is another thing to say, 'Lord, I confess that I was unkind to Jane this morning, selfish with Tom this afternoon, *etc*.' Allow the Holy Spirit to search your heart and to reveal to you the failings of the immediate past. On occasions it might be valuable to read 1 Corinthians 13:4-7, 'Love is patient and kind . . .', substituting 'I' for 'love', and seeing how far you get before the Spirit reveals to you how unloving you may have been during the past day or two. After all, the basis of sin is selfishness, which is the opposite of love. Having confessed our sins, we need to believe the clear promise that God forgives completely: 'I will remember their sins and their misdeeds no more.'[5] God never wants us to stay guilty; as soon as we confess our guilt he releases us from our debt. This is how our love for him grows. It is when we are forgiven much that we can love much.

Thanksgiving Like every parent I constantly train my children to say 'Thank you'. Ingratitude is a

[3] 1 John 3:18   [4] Psalm 66:18
[5] Hebrews 10:17; *cf.* 1 John 1:7, 9; *etc.*

wretched, destructive factor in relationships. As soon as a married couple take each other for granted, trouble sets in. So it is with God. David, in Psalm 103, once told himself to 'forget not all his benefits', and then he went on to list some of the gifts of God's love that he had received: forgiveness, healing, freedom, love, mercy, satisfaction, life, strength, guidance, faithfulness. If prayer becomes dull, or if you feel discouraged or depressed, consciously start thanking God for all the positive aspects of your life and situation, and even for his promised control in your trials and difficulties. Genuine gratitude is a marvellous way of healing and strengthening all relationships, not least our relationship with God.

Supplication Be definite in your prayer requests. 'Nothing is too great for his power; nothing is too small for his love.' Needless anxiety is caused when we fail to tell God about the details that trouble us. 'You do not have, because you do not ask,' wrote James.[6] And Paul, in a magnificent passage about rejoicing in the Lord and being filled with his peace, told the Christians at Philippi to 'have no anxiety about *anything*, but in *everything* by prayer and supplication with thanksgiving let your requests be made known to God. And (then, if you do that) the peace of God, which passes all understanding, will keep your hearts and your minds in Christ Jesus.'[7] This form of prayer is like unpacking a suitcase. Many people are worn out by the heavy burdens they have to carry. Worry today is a killer. But in prayer we should unpack that suitcase, and bring each need before our

[6] James 4:2   [7] Philippians 4:6, 7

heavenly Father: 'Lord, here is my work ... and my family ... and my need for guidance.' As one Dutch Christian, Corrie ten Boom, once put it, 'Travel with a round face and an empty suitcase!'

We must therefore listen to God, primarily through the Bible, and speak to God in prayer. It is important, however, to stress one practical point. Although our personal relationship with God must be developed, and must be based mainly on a *personal* time for Bible study and prayer, requiring a quiet place and a suitable time (first thing in the morning is best for most people—get an effective alarm clock!), there is no doubt that the first Christians met frequently *together*, and worshipped together and studied together and prayed together.[8] It is when two or three are gathered together in the name of Jesus that he is especially in their midst.[9] For those used to studying books, a private time of Bible study and prayer should present no special problems, and this would be extremely valuable as well as any group activity. But for those with a non-academic background who find such study especially difficult, or for those under particular pressures (such as mothers of young children), it may well be that corporate study and prayer is by far the most profitable. God speaks to us through one another. It is 'together with God's people' that we 'may have the power to understand how broad and long and high and deep is Christ's love'.[1] Each of us on our own may see only one facet of the diamond of God's truth. It is only together that we begin to comprehend the whole. Try then to assess (maybe with the help of an

[8] See, *e.g.*, Acts 2:42–47   [9] Matthew 18:20
[1] Ephesians 3:18 (TEV)

37

older Christian) what is the most valuable way for *you* to develop your relationship with God. What is right for one Christian may not be right for another. The balance between private and corporate study, the method to be used, the time given to prayer, the use of prayer lists—these and many other factors will vary from Christian to Christian. Although we can often stimulate and challenge one another by what we have found helpful, we should never be in bondage to the pattern of another person's devotional life—providing that we honestly do not use this as an excuse for laziness.

Most people, for the first few months after their commitment to Christ, find it of special value to link up with one other Christian who is spiritually older in the faith. Humanly speaking I doubt if I would have survived without this regular, personal help. I met with another Christian virtually every week for several months, and together we read appropriate passages in the Bible and talked about many subjects, doctrinal and practical. I was thoroughly confused with a tangle of religious and philosophical ideas in my head, and my whole way of life needed a new direction altogether. This detailed, personal counsel, therefore, proved quite invaluable. Seek out such a friend, of the same sex and with some clear understanding of the basic truths of the gospel. You may be able to share openly and honestly with such a person in a way that would be more difficult in a group.

5 Not alone

'Come to Jesus, to that living stone,' wrote Peter,
'... and like living stones be yourselves built into a
spiritual house.'[1] If you find a gaping hole in a wall of
a building, and a pile of stones from that wall scattered
on the ground nearby, not only are those stones in the
wrong place and useless on their own, but the rest of
the building is seriously weakened by their absence.
So it is with the Christian and the church.

The two commonest metaphors for the church in
the Bible are the building of God and the body of
Christ: 'You are ... God's building;' 'You are God's
temple;' 'You are the body of Christ.'[2] The primary
purpose of both metaphors is to stress our unity in
Christ: we need one another, we belong to one another, we are joined together. As soon as a person
belongs to Christ he belongs to the body of Christ.
Although the Christian faith is a personal faith, it is
never a private faith. It is impossible to claim that
you belong to God and to Christ without at the same

[1] 1 Peter 2: 4, 5   [2] 1 Corinthians 3: 9, 16; 12: 27

39

time becoming a stone in God's building and a member of Christ's body. Indeed the effectiveness of the early church can be summed up in two striking sentences: 'Those who believed were of one heart and soul, and ... they had everything in common. And with great power the apostles gave their testimony to the resurrection of the Lord Jesus, and great grace was upon them all.'[3] The New Testament knows nothing of solitary Christianity. An independent spirit is the spirit of the world, and not of Christ. Significantly we are told that 'the Lord added to their number (= the church) day by day those who were being saved'.[4]

Determine, then, to find your place within the local fellowship of Christians where you are, certainly in a local church and also, if applicable, in the Christian Union of your college, school, factory, unit, or office. You may not find it easy, initially. When Saul of Tarsus met with the living Christ he at once attempted to get involved with the local body of Christ. But he was given a cool and negative reception. They doubted his conversion and were suspicious of his motives. And there were other natural barriers, too. Saul was a gifted intellectual, highly educated and influential, a Jewish leader and a Roman citizen: his pedigree was impeccable. Humanly speaking it could not have been easy for him to have joined a despised minority group consisting of poor, illiterate fishermen and those who once were cheats, traitors, prostitutes and thieves. Moreover Saul had hated and persecuted this Christian 'sect' with persistent and skilful ruthlessness. And now he had changed sides! Indeed it

[3] Acts 4:32, 33   [4] Acts 2:47

40

was this social, religious, and intellectual aristocrat who later wrote: 'There is neither Jew nor Greek, there is neither slave nor free, there is neither male nor female; for you are all one in Christ Jesus.'[5]

Therefore, even if your natural reaction to, or from, your local group of Christians is cool, and even if there are marked social, cultural, racial, and intellectual differences, realize that, with them, you *belong* to God's building and Christ's body. You need them, and they need you. You simply cannot do without each other;[6] and the more you get involved with other Christians, the more real God will become in your life. 'No man has ever seen God,' wrote John; 'if we love one another, God abides in us.'[7] Aim to be as committed to other Christians as you are to Christ. See Christ in your brother-in-Christ: 'As you did it to one of the least of these my brethren, you did it to me,' said Jesus.[8]

Sadly not all churches are alive with the Spirit of Christ. There is an urgent need for spiritual renewal throughout the world, and the church has often rightly deserved the nickname of 'God's frozen people'. Therefore discover a church where its members really have found this new life in Christ, where the Scriptures are taught and applied, where there is worship and warmth. Sometimes this warmth will be found in the church's youth group, or in a home Bible study group, rather than in the main Sunday services. Although you should join in with the public worship, identifying yourself with God's people in that place, you may find the smaller groups more immediately

[5] Galatians 3:28 [6] See 1 Corinthians 12:12–27
[7] 1 John 4:12 [8] See Matthew 25:31–46

helpful. Ask an older Christian if you need guidance about this.

Even if you spend a little time locating a helpful church, make sure you join it and become fully involved in its life and worship. Don't be a touch-line spectator or a religious critic. Every church, you will discover, has its faults—often obvious and glaring ones. It is inevitably a fellowship of sinners. It has often been said that if you do find a perfect church, don't join it, for then it would cease to be perfect! There is only one way to bring more life to a church: give *your* life! Spiritually we must die before others can live.[9] 'By this we know love, that he laid down his life for us: and we ought to lay down our lives for the brethren.'[1] A community of love is what every true church should be like. Such love is undoubtedly costly, but how enormously relevant is a loving fellowship of Christians when the greatest problem today is loneliness, and when there is such a universal breakdown in human relationships.

If you are a university or college student, then your degree of involvement with a local church, both in term and vacation, will need some careful thought. You should clearly be involved with other Christian students; you have a unique responsibility to witness to your Christian faith in your student circles, and therefore the balance between your commitment to a Christian Union and your commitment to a local church will need to be worked out carefully and wisely. Each situation is different; but the degree to which you share your life with other Christians will largely determine the degree of God's blessing in your

[9] See John 12:24   [1] 1 John 3:16

life. 'How good and pleasant it is when brothers dwell in unity! ... For there the Lord has commanded the blessing.'[2]

The spiritual principles of our common life together in Christ are perfectly illustrated by the common meal that Jesus told us to share together, the Lord's Supper or Holy Communion. The bread and the wine are symbols of the body of Christ broken for us on the cross and his blood poured out for our sins, and they also express our unity as Christians: 'Because there is one bread, we who are many are one body, for we all partake of the one bread.'[3] At this service we look in four directions. We *look back*, and remember with thanksgiving Christ's once-for-all death for our sins; we *look in* and examine ourselves, so that we do not eat and drink 'in an unworthy manner' but in a true attitude of repentance and faith; we *look around* and realize that we share together the death and resurrection of Christ, and through this we have now become 'one body'; and we *look forward* to the promised heavenly banquet, of which the Lord's Supper is a shadow and pledge. We are to 'proclaim the Lord's death until he comes'.[4] It is for this reason that the service of Holy Communion has rightly taken the central place in Christian worship through the world. It is there, especially, that we are to 'feed on him in our hearts by faith, with thanksgiving'.

Further, as members of Christ's body we are called to serve one another, just as he came 'not to be served but to serve'. Far too many Christians go to church to *receive* the help and teaching and encouragement that

[2] Psalm 133:1, 3 [3] 1 Corinthians 10:17
[4] See 1 Corinthians 11:23, 24

they need. Certainly we must receive, otherwise we have nothing to give. But the more we give, the more we receive. And the spirit of service is the spirit of the Master who gathered up the towel to wash the feet of his disciples.[5] Further, Paul's constant stress[6] is that the gifts given to us by God have been given to be shared, in order to build up and strengthen the whole body of Christ: 'Having gifts that differ according to the grace given to us, *let us use them*.' He goes on to describe a rich variety of gifts: prophecy, service, teaching, exhortation, giving, helping, compassion, wisdom, knowledge, faith, healing, miracle-working, distinguishing between spirits, speaking in tongues, interpreting tongues, administration, evangelism, pastoral counsel, *etc*. There is nothing to suggest that even this list is complete. No doubt we could add the more 'natural' gifts (although they all ultimately come from God) such as music, drama, art, electrical skills, typing, printing, writing, dancing, joinery, plumbing, agriculture, and a good many more. If any gift is really used to glorify Christ and to edify the body of Christ it is a gift of the Holy Spirit. The vital point is that we must learn to serve one another in love: 'As each has received a gift, employ it for one another.'[7] Being totally committed to a local fellowship of Christians—and, more widely, to the whole church of God—is an essential expression of unselfish self-sacrificing love, which is the primary hallmark of a true disciple of Jesus Christ.

[5] John 13:1–20
[6] *E.g.* Romans 12; 1 Corinthians 12; Ephesians 4
[7] 1 Peter 4:10

6 Reproducing

We have already thought briefly of our responsibility as Christians in the world in which we live—God's world. Every area of life matters to him. Problems of pollution, over-population, oppression of minority groups, inequalities, and injustices: all these, and more, are a vital concern to a God who is pure and loving and just; and therefore they must also become the concern of God's people. When Christians form a religious ghetto, opting out of the immense responsibilities facing man today, they have also departed from the compassion of their heavenly Father, who is the Creator of the whole earth.

There is, however, one particular area where Christians have a special responsibility in the world: sharing the good news of Jesus Christ. 'You are ... God's own people, that you may declare the wonderful deeds of him who called you out of darkness into his marvellous light.'[1] The Archbishop of York has described modern society's worst problem not as inflation,

[1] 1 Peter 2:9

but as 'the burden of meaninglessness. This is a wasting, enervating disease far worse than inflation.' Most psychiatrists have for years been saying the same thing. Man is groping in the darkness, having lost his bearings and sense of direction. It is partly for this reason that the claim of Jesus to be the light of the world is of the utmost relevance: 'The people who walked in darkness have seen a great light.'[2]

Moreover Christ's disciples, too, are called 'the light of the world',[3] and it is part of our Christian commission to show others the light of Christ. God's light comes to us especially through his Word, which is a lamp to our feet and a light to our path.[4] In order to fulfil our responsibilities in the world, therefore, it is necessary to know the truth of the gospel and to be able to communicate it simply and clearly to others. And in doing this, hardly anything shines so brightly as a life which reflects the love and joy of Jesus.

Not every Christian is called to be an evangel*ist*, but all Christians must be involved in evangel*ism*, which is the primary task of the church, next to worship. 'To evangelize is to spread the good news that Jesus Christ died for our sins and was raised from the dead according to the Scriptures, and that as the reigning Lord he now offers the forgiveness of sins and the liberating gift of the Spirit to all who repent and believe.'[5]

To begin with, you may feel that there is nothing you can say because you have only just started yourself. Even from your first day as a Christian, however,

---

[2] Isaiah 9:2   [3] Matthew 5:14   [4] Psalm 119:105
[5] Quoted from the Lausanne Covenant, resulting from the International Congress on Evangelization, 1974.

there is plenty that you can do to share your new-found faith in Christ. Let me give a few suggestions.

1. Prayer Start praying for two or three friends, every day if possible, asking God to make himself known to them as he did to you. Pray that they may understand their need of Jesus. Pray that the Spirit may guide you so that you can see what you can do to help them to find him. I have often prayed a prayer like this: 'Lord, give me eyes to see, and grace to seize, every opportunity for you.' It is often said that our best work as Christians might well be talking to God about people, rather than talking to people about God. Write down today a few names of those for whom you are going to pray.

2. 'Come and see' This is a wonderful method of evangelism. In the first chapter of John's Gospel we see several men finding Christ in this way. Jesus said to two of them 'Come and see'; and off went one of them to say to his own brother, Simon Peter, in effect, 'Come and see.' Later Philip tried to convince Nathanael. He could not answer Nathanael's sceptical objections, so he simply said 'Come and see'—which is precisely what Nathanael did. Later, in the fourth chapter, a Samaritan woman, having met Jesus herself, went off at once to tell all her friends, 'Come, see a man who told me all that I ever did. Can this be the Christ?' And lots of her friends and acquaintances came and believed. At that stage the woman could not possibly have explained her faith to anyone, but many found Christ by this method of 'come and see'.

You can do the same. Ask people to come to special

services (guest services or evangelistic services); indeed use ordinary services, especially if the local church is a lively one; invite friends to any Christian meeting which may be appropriate; introduce someone to an older Christian friend who could explain the faith more clearly than you. 'Come and see'—*anyone* can say that!

3. Personal experience Tell others how you found Christ. What brought you to this point? What steps did you take? What difference has it made? It is not so much what you say but the way that you say it. The reality of your experience, and the fact that something has happened, will speak for itself, even if you cannot answer all the questions which may be raised. John tells us that 'many Samaritans from that city believed in him (Jesus) because of the woman's testimony'. We are to be witnesses, and a witness must testify to personal experience. Many a person has found Christ through the testimony of a Christian, however inexperienced that Christian might be.

4. Literature Helpful books and booklets are increasingly numerous today. Choose one that you have read yourself, and try to assess what will be meaningful for the friend you are trying to help. Various paperbacks[6] spell out the heart of the Christian faith for those who are searching for something; others give more of the reality of God in the lives of Christians today;[7] others

---

[6] Such as *Jesus Spells Freedom, Man Alive!* or *Runaway World* by Michael Green (all IVP), or *My God is Real* or *In Search of God* by David Watson (both Falcon).

[7] Such as *God's Smuggler* by Brother Andrew, or *The Hiding Place* by Corrie ten Boom (both Hodder and Stoughton).

are booklets which explain the steps to Christ for those who want to know 'just how'.[8] God is clearly using literature of this kind to bring people all over the world to a living faith in Christ. Keep a stock of these books and booklets handy. Use them whenever you detect that the interest is sufficient for that book to be read. And then pray hard! After a time discover what has been the reaction to the book. Has he read it? What does he think about it? Would he like to find Christ for himself? Gently press home the need to do something about it.

5. *Conversation* Much of the recorded ministry of Jesus is personal conversation with individuals, and you can pray that God will help you to do this as you go on as a Christian. Read some of the incidents in the Gospels and Acts, and see what you can learn. For example, see how Jesus dealt with the Samaritan woman in John 4. First of all he *established contact*. It wasn't easy: he was a Jew, she was a Samaritan; he was a man, she was a woman. On both scores a conversation in public was definitely not done! Love will always find a way somehow, however, and Jesus asked her gently for a favour: 'Give me a drink.' Next, he *aroused her curiosity* by telling her that he could give her living water which could quench her thirst. We can do the same by talking of our own experience, by lending a book, or simply by saying 'Come and see'. Jesus then *touched a sore spot* by asking her to call her husband. As she had lived with six men this was a decidedly delicate issue. But Jesus knew that she must

[8] Such as *Becoming a Christian* by John R. W. Stott (IVP), or *Journey into Life* by Norman Warren (Falcon).

sort out her wrong relationships with men before she could find a right relationship with God. Next, he *avoided a red herring*. Embarrassed by his reference to her casual sex-life, she raised a theological diversion: where should people worship—in Samaria or in Jerusalem? Jesus dealt briefly with her question, but brought her back to a spiritual issue: 'True worshippers will worship the Father in spirit and truth.' Finally, he *brought her to a decision*. Although she tried familiar delaying tactics, Jesus made her face up to her response to him there and then.

Study carefully this story and the ways of handling a conversation. You will be amazed by the relevance of it all as you try to talk with your own friends. Try soon to learn a simple framework of verses so that you know how to answer someone who is, in effect, asking the question, How can God become real in my life? Read again the first chapter of this book for one way in which you can answer that question. Another simple framework that I have frequently used (with variations) is this:

Admit your need: Romans 3:23; 6:23; Isaiah 59:2

Believe that Christ died for you: Isaiah 53:6; 1 Peter 3:18

Count the cost: Mark 8:34–38

Invite Christ into your life: John 1:12; Revelation 3:20

Write out these verses; try to learn them; put the references in the back of your Bible; and pray for opportunities for telling others how to find Christ. I had the privilege of going through very similar verses about three weeks after I had found Christ myself. I expect I explained it all very badly; but something went home. I then said, 'Come and see a friend of mine who can explain it better'; and very soon that person had committed his life to Christ. I could hardly sleep for joy.

Remember that God's truth is spiritual truth. Be much in prayer, asking the Holy Spirit to cause a person to 'see' the truth with his heart and spirit, and not just his mind. A. W. Tozer once wrote that 'for a man to understand revealed truth requires an act of God equal to the original act which inspired the text (of the Bible)'. In other words, to give a person understanding is the sovereign work of the Spirit of God. When we seek to share our faith with others we shall often feel the full force of Christ's words, 'Apart from me you can do nothing.'[9] Human rhetoric and the techniques of persuasion are totally useless. Paul ruthlessly eschewed all dependence on 'oratory and human wisdom' in his preaching, in order that 'the Holy Spirit's power (might be) in my words, proving to those who heard them that the message was from God'.[1]

Be willing to learn from mistakes, and pray frequently for the courage to talk about Jesus, and indeed for the privilege of doing so. There is no more exciting, demanding, and rewarding work in the world than winning men and women for Christ.

Another practical way in which you can help, especially if you are a student or teacher, is by taking part in the numerous Christian camps, houseparties, and other holiday activities that happen each year, mainly

[9] John 15:5   [1] 1 Corinthians 2:1–5 (Living Bible)

in the summer but also at Easter. Holidays and vacations, instead of being filled up with basically selfish pursuits, can be most profitably used in direct Christian service. During five years at university I went to a large number of boys' camps; and these led many boys to Christ (a good proportion of whom are in active Christian work today) and also provided a first-rate training ground for my own ministry in later years. As Christians, our time and energies belong to the Lord, and we must not waste the gifts and opportunities that God has given us.

A communist once threw down this challenge to a Christian: 'The gospel is a much more powerful weapon for the renewal of society than is our Marxist philosophy, but all the same it is *we* who will finally beat *you*.... We communists do not play with words. We are realists, and seeing that we are determined to achieve our object, we know how to obtain the means. Of our salaries and wages we keep only what is strictly necessary, and we give up our free time and part of our holidays. You, however, give only a little time and hardly any money for the spreading of the gospel of Christ. How can anybody believe in the supreme value of the gospel if you do not practise it, if you do not spread it, if you sacrifice neither time nor money for it? ... We believe in our communist message, and we are ready to sacrifice everything, even our life.... But you people are afraid to soil your hands.' Small wonder that the communists have swallowed up one third of the world in half a century!

7 Chosen to serve

No man is an island, and Jesus taught that serving others is the mark of true Christian discipleship. He told his disciples repeatedly that he himself had come to *serve*. Whilst they sometimes foolishly argued amongst themselves about who was the greatest, Jesus, taking the place of a menial servant, washed their feet. Always he loved them, cared for them, sought the best for them, and eventually laid down his own life that they—and we—might live.

In practical terms this commitment to service should affect our attitude at *home*. Unless you know that your parents, or husband or wife, will understand and appreciate your new relationship with Christ, don't say too much too soon. Many new Christians have created numerous and unnecessary complications for themselves by talking or writing hastily and enthusiastically about their new-found faith. Such enthusiasm will very likely be misunderstood or mistrusted, and it is hard to avoid the impression that you are preaching at that person if he does not yet share your convictions. Existing human relationships may seem threatened, especially in the case of husband and wife; and our efforts to share Christ with our family may be taken to mean that we no longer love them as they are but only as we would like them to be.

The answer to all this is to demonstrate the reality of Christ by a new spirit of service; by being thoughtful and helpful, gentle and considerate. It is often the small practical actions that speak most loudly: doing the washing up, taking out the bins, cleaning the house, putting the kids to bed, weeding the garden, keeping your room tidy, getting the tea ready. In a world marked by selfishness a sensitivity to the needs of others, and love in little things, can make all the difference. When Paul wrote his magnificent chapter on love, and explained that love is 'patient and kind', he was effectively drawing a portrait of Christ. This, then, is how Christ will be most clearly seen in our homes.

Unfortunately Christians often find that the home is the most difficult place in which to live for Jesus. Those we live with know us too well, they see all the cracks in our character. Home, of course, is where we naturally relax. If, however, we relax spiritually and neglect our relationship with Christ, our self-life will go on a spree, and our family will be unimpressed by our Christian profession. It is important, therefore, to make some disciplined time for Bible reading and prayer, and, if possible, for Christian fellowship. But in doing this don't cut yourself off from your family; rather pray specifically that your time spent with them will somehow reflect the love and gentleness of Christ. This will speak volumes. Ignatius of Antioch wrote 1800 years ago: 'It is better to keep silence and to be, than to talk and not to be.'

We have also a new responsibility to our *work*. The New Testament recognizes no sharp distinction between the 'spiritual' and the 'secular'. Indeed, in the context of eating and drinking Paul wrote, 'Whatever you do, do all to the glory of God.'[1] If Jesus were to correct your essay, read your typing, sit at your table, watch your machine—would it alter your work, or your attitude to work? 'Whatever you do, in word or deed, do everything in the name of the Lord Jesus.'[2] Every task can be 'for Jesus'; and we should, as Christians, develop better relationships with others at work and with those who are over us: 'Be obedient to your earthly masters ... as to Christ; not in the way of eye-service, as men-pleasers, but as servants of Christ, doing the will of God from the heart, rendering service with a good will as to the Lord.'[3] Paul wrote that to slaves who knew nothing of a fair day's pay for a fair day's work, or the protection of trades unions, or social benefits and sick benefits and bonuses and overtime and holidays and the comparative affluence of most working people today. Yet even in their situation their work could be done as for Christ.

Today it is honesty and reliability in little things that count for so much. The fact that you hand your essays in on time, or come punctually to work, or refrain from pilfering office equipment, or keep your conversation healthy, will soon mark you out as a disciple of Christ. Refusing to fiddle the accounts or knock things off at work will not make you popular; but it will bring Christ into a situation where he will be largely unknown. A Cambridge hockey 'blue' once

[1] 1 Corinthians 10:31 [2] Colossians 3:17 [3] Ephesians 6:5-7

told me of the considerable respect he had for a Christian in the hockey team. In passing he explained that the rest of the team felt that, when this Christian was with them, they could not tell the sort of jokes and stories they usually told. Jesus once said that we were to be the salt of the earth, and it is part of the property of salt that it stops meat and other food from going bad.

Christians have a responsibility also in the *society* in which they live. What are the social needs of the sick and lonely? Are there areas of injustice or hardship which are crying out for someone to do something? And having discerned some of those needs, what does God want you to do about them? Where should you concentrate your time and energies? Organizations such as Shelter or the Samaritans are frequently in need of voluntary helpers. There are many local Christian groups, too, which are seeking to meet the needs of young people, alcoholics, ex-prisoners and the physically or mentally handicapped. Although the welfare state, where it exists, has relieved immense suffering, the very real needs of individuals, families, immigrants, or whole sections of society, are crying out for urgent help. Christians have no right to talk about the love of God unless, in some measure at least, they are prepared to show that God in his love really cares about people, whatever their colour, creed or culture.

Of course it is possible to plunge so whole-heartedly into some social concern that you miss out on Christian fellowship and teaching, which are essential to spiritual growth. More than anything, our relationship with God must not be neglected. At the same time John rightly observes that 'if any one has the world's goods and sees his brother in need, yet closes his heart against him, how does God's love abide in him? ... Let us not love in word or speech but in deed and in truth.'[4] In fact when Jesus spelt out the two great commandments, loving God and loving your neighbour, he went on to illustrate what loving your neighbour could mean. He told the story of a man attacked and wounded by thieves, subsequently ignored by the religious professionals who 'passed by on the other side', and eventually cared for by a stranger from Samaria.[5] The punch of this story lay not only in the failure to love people on the part of those who professed to love God, but in the loving care of the Jew by a Samaritan, when Jews and Samaritans were in racial conflict with each other. This practical love for people is an essential expression of our love for God.

Also, of course, Christians are a part of God's *world*. We cannot therefore opt out of the responsibility we have towards the hungry and the oppressed. Sometimes the needs seem to be so impossibly vast that apathy sets in: 'What can *I* do about it anyway?' In fact there is much that an individual can do, if he is willing to show sacrificial love for others. Christian action groups, such as TEAR Fund and Christian Aid, bring excellent practical help to some of the distressed areas of the world, and they have a variety of schemes to stimulate interest and support here at home. Various missionary societies offer shorter or longer terms of service abroad for those who are willing to work without pay or with only the barest expenses covered. Many have found such work demanding but enor-

[4] 1 John 3:17, 18   [5] Luke 10:27–37

mously enriching, especially when done consciously for Jesus. Developing an intelligent and prayerful concern for a missionary, or missionary society or overseas project, can also prove immensely valuable, and this will avoid the danger of being too preoccupied with a narrow sphere of work at home. Indeed there is no end to the exciting openings for Christians who believe in the living God, whose eyes are open to the needs of the world, whose hearts are full of the compassion of Christ, and who have kept awake their sense of responsibility.

8 Why doubt?

Several weeks after committing my life to Christ I wrote in a small diary, 'Is it all true, or am I making it up?' Virtually every Christian has moments, or even prolonged periods, of real doubt; and the first wave of doubt may come very soon after the initial honeymoon period, or even earlier if the spiritual 'honeymoon' does not live up to expectations. If you have fairly recently become a Christian you may be battling with your faith even now, believing one moment and doubting the next.

What are the causes of doubt? There are several.

1. Temptation In the first recorded temptation in the Old Testament, the devil whispered to Eve, 'Did God say ...?'[1] Here is the oldest and most effective temptation of all: trying to make someone doubt God's word. In the first recorded temptation in the New Testament, we find the same trick: 'If you are the Son of God ... If you are the Son of God ...'[2] These

[1] Genesis 3:1   [2] Matthew 4:3, 6

subtle doubts came to Jesus very soon after God the Father had assured him, 'This is my beloved Son.'[3] It is much the same with us today. God's word is quite clear: if I ask Jesus into my life, he *will* come in; if he comes, he will never leave; if he gives me eternal life, I shall *never* perish; nothing can separate me from God's love. Jesus, however, called Satan the Father of lies; and back he comes with his old tricks: 'If you are a Christian, why don't you feel different? If Christ is with you, why don't you experience his presence? If he has given you a new life, why are you so very much the same? If ... if ... if ...' As we have already seen, the best answer to these temptations is to go back to the changeless and powerful Word of God: 'It is written ...' As we meditate on God's promises our flagging faith will revive, and as we use God's Word to counter these doubts, the devil will flee from us.[4]

2. *Disobedience* When a person commits his life to Christ he begins a new relationship and a new friendship. The new relationship is fixed: even on a human level we cannot cease to be a child of our parents, however strained that relationship might become. The new friendship, though, is a much more delicate matter, and needs constant watching. When that friendship is spoilt through disobedience and sin we can lose the enjoyment and awareness of our relationship with God, even though that relationship is in fact unbroken. When God's people felt cut off from God, Isaiah the prophet gave them the straightforward explanation: 'Your sins have hid his face from you so that he does not hear.'[5] When king David had dis-

obeyed God he cried out, 'Cast me not away from thy presence.... Restore to me the joy of thy salvation.'[6] He had lost, not God's salvation, but the joy of it.

Often doubts emerge as a result of wrong relationships. If we hold on to resentments, anger, bitterness or lack of forgiveness, God may seem a million miles away. If a relationship with a boyfriend or girlfriend is not the best, similar doubts may occur. When it comes to close and intimate friendships, maybe leading to marriage, the Bible is insistent that all such relationships must be formed in Christ: 'Don't be teamed with those who do not love the Lord, for what do the people of God have in common with the people of sin? ... How can a Christian be a partner with one who doesn't believe?'[7] Strong words indeed, but there have been more spiritual shipwrecks from relationships that are not 'in Christ' than from probably any other cause.

3. Ignorance Jesus once said, 'The truth will make you free,'[8] and nowhere is this more clearly seen in experience than in the area of doubt. A Swiss pastor observed, 'It is remarkable to note the ignorance of most believers concerning the forgiveness of their sins.... When one speaks of an actual personal certainty, and when one asks the direct question, "Do you know, now, if your sins are forgiven?" nine times out of ten their reply is evasive.... Can one be surprised, then, that the faith of our church members is so

[6] Psalm 51:11, 12
[7] 2 Corinthians 6:14, 15 (Living Bible)
[8] John 8:32

dull?'[9] That is why Paul took such care to teach the young churches to whom he was writing. His letters contain many practical instructions about living as sons of God; but he also gave detailed doctrinal teaching so that the Christians could really *understand* the riches of God's grace and their inheritance in Christ as sons of God. Most of their personal and relationship problems were due to their ignorance of their position in Christ, or to their failure to remember it. Again and again Paul says to his readers: 'Do you not know ...? We know ... We know ... So you also must consider yourselves ...'[1]

Throughout the New Testament there are numerous warnings about false teachers and prophets. We are to 'test the spirits to see whether they are of God; for many false prophets have gone out into the world'.[2] The surest and safest test of any teaching is to discover whether or not it is in accordance with the Scriptures. Jesus rebuked some of the religious teachers of his day because of their departures from the Scriptures.[3] Once we leave the rock of God's Word we shall soon be tossed to and fro on the winds and seas of doubt. Paul urged the Ephesian Christians not to be 'children, tossed to and fro with every wind of doctrine';[4] and he counselled the leader of that church, Timothy, to 'preach the word, ... be unfailing in patience and in teaching' because of the persistent danger of false teaching.[5]

Together with Bible teaching and study, there are numerous Christian books available, many of which

[9] *Healing for you* by Bernard Martin (Lutterworth), p. 37.
[1] See Romans 6:1–11 [2] 1 John 4:1
[3] See Matthew 22:29; Mark 7:6–13 [4] Ephesians 4:14
[5] 2 Timothy 4:1–4

are enormously helpful for an increased understanding of God, his gifts to us in Christ, and the reality of the Holy Spirit in the lives of people today. A healthy balance of books will be best, mixing doctrinal, devotional, practical and biographical together, so that we are neither choked by a surfeit of tough theological meat, nor sickened by the soufflés of spiritual experiences. A balanced diet is necessary for the healthy Christian.

4. Loneliness Christians are not meant to be alone but in close fellowship with other Christians where they can share and bear one another's problems. If the loneliness is unavoidable then God promises that his grace will be sufficient for us, even if the time is a testing one. But so much loneliness is self-imposed. Perhaps we neglect some fellowship that we could have, such as a local church or Christian Union, and in that case we have only ourselves to blame for the spiritual battles we face, for we are told specifically in the Bible not to neglect to meet together, but rather to encourage one another and exhort one another 'every day'.[6] Or perhaps we do join up with other Christians, but fail to share our problems with them. This denies the whole purpose of fellowship, which means 'sharing'. Anyway, shut in on ourselves and alone with our thoughts, we open our minds wide to doubts and depressions of all kinds. John Wesley once said, 'Remember you cannot serve him alone; you must, therefore, find companions, or make them; the Bible knows nothing of solitary religion.' Indeed so crucial was Christian fellowship in the New Testament

[6] Hebrews 10:25; 3:13

church, that the severest discipline, reserved for the worst of immoral or blasphemous offences, was to exclude the offender from the fellowship. This amounted to delivering the person to Satan, since there would no longer be the protection and strength of other Christians until that person was brought to repentance.[7] Our relationships with Christ and with the body of Christ are virtually inseparable.

5. *Inactivity* Many writers have commented on the striking contrast between the Sea of Galilee and the Dead Sea in Palestine, even though the two are directly linked by the river Jordan with only some 60 or 70 miles between them. The Sea of Galilee is fresh and alive, but the Dead Sea is so deadly in its salt, potash, magnesium and calcium chloride contents that no fish or plant could begin to survive. Why the marked difference? The answer is simple. The Sea of Galilee is constantly receiving fresh water from the north, and from the surrounding hills, and fresh water is all the time flowing out towards the south. But the Dead Sea is a dead end. Fresh water comes in, but nothing flows out. It simply evaporates, leaving the chemical deposits.

The point of the illustration should be obvious. A healthy Christian life will have constant outlets in loving service and active witness. The living water of the Spirit therefore flows in, and flows out again, keeping the Christian spiritually fresh. But if a Christian ignores direct Christian service and comes to church and meetings only to receive, then soon that life will become stagnant and unhealthy, leaving large

[7] See 1 Corinthians 5 : 3–5

deadly deposits of doubt and probably other complications as well.

6. *Confusion* A Christian may find himself questioning some of his most basic beliefs when he is thrown into confusion, usually in one of two areas in his life. The first concerns *guidance*. If he genuinely believes that God guided him in some direction, for example the choice of a wife or a job or a house, and he later feels that it was all a big mistake—what then? Did God hear his prayer? Is there a God to hear any prayer? It is easy to see how such nagging questions can gnaw away at the foundations of our faith. Part of the muddle is often caused by confusion over the means of guidance.[8] Rather like navigation lights, we normally need more than one sign before we can discern God's leading in our life. Hasty decisions are nearly always wrong, especially when they involve some major course of action in the future. God frequently uses many different ways of speaking to us: circumstances, the counsel of other Christians, the wisdom of his written Word in the Scriptures and prayer. We need to have a sense of peace in our hearts over some matter, and be willing to wait until the fog has lifted and the peaceful light of Christ's presence is there: 'The peace that Christ gives is to be the judge in your hearts.'[9] We should also be willing for our decisions to be tested by other Christians who may see the issue from a different point of view; and indeed be willing to make mistakes and to learn from our

[8] I have looked at this more fully in my book *One in the Spirit*, pp. 54–61 (Hodder and Stoughton). See also the booklet *Guidance* by O. R. Barclay (IVP).

[9] Colossians 3:15 (TEV)

mistakes. It could be presumption ('The Lord *has* told me') or pride ('I'm sure the Lord *did* tell me—') that rocks the boat of our faith: we claim too much and refuse to admit mistakes. In Acts 16 Paul and Timothy tried to go into Phrygia and Galatia, and then into Bithynia; but one way or another the way was blocked. Then Paul, through a vision, sensed that they were being called to Macedonia instead. This is what they eventually did, concluding that God had so guided them. But guidance for them was not a simple matter. It very seldom is. We are not to use God as a heavenly computer; rather, in matters of guidance we are often thrown into a new humble dependence on him because of the difficulties of it all. And this in itself is a good thing.

The second area of confusion is that of seemingly *unanswered prayer*, perhaps concerning sickness or suffering. When Job went through a period of intense suffering and God seemed strangely silent, he also experienced a ruthless questioning of all his cherished beliefs: 'Oh, that I knew where I might find him!'[1] God, of course, had not been inactive, but often delays in answering prayer are necessary to test our faith, to humble our pride, to break our self-righteousness, to correct our relationships, to equip us for future service or to do other deep works in our lives which cannot be done when everything is running smoothly. In fact these testing-times are nearly always times when God is doing his most profound work. We may be much more aware of the darkness and silence and pain, but we have to accept by faith that 'in *everything* God works for good with those who love him'.[2] Nothing is

[1] Job 23:3   [2] Romans 8:28

outside the control of his loving purposes for us, even if we are totally unable to see that at the time.

7. *Ingratitude* One of the most striking features of the New Testament is the strong thread of thanksgiving and praise on almost every page, even though many of those first Christians suffered intense hardship, poverty, and persecution. Paul referred sometimes to what he had suffered for Christ: imprisonments, countless beatings, stonings, shipwrecks, hunger and thirst, cold and exposure.[3] Yet throughout his Letters we hear this persistent note of thanksgiving: 'Always and for everything giving thanks ... Rejoice in the Lord always ... Be thankful ... Give thanks in all circumstances ...'[4] By this constant thanksgiving and praise Paul experienced the constant renewal of God's Spirit in his life. The love of Christ went on and on being poured into his heart.

The opposite, however, is also true. Ingratitude can rob a Christian of the experience of God's love almost more quickly than anything else. The Christian's first duty is to worship God, and there are bound to be problems if we neglect to do this. We may not always feel like praising God; but in that case we offer him the 'sacrifice of praise'.[5] We praise him because he is God and is always worthy of our praise, even if that involves a real effort on our part. 'Great is the Lord and (therefore) greatly to be praised!'[6] Certainly the tonic of thanksgiving is one of the greatest antidotes to doubt.

[3] See 2 Corinthians 11:23–28
[4] See Ephesians 5:20; Philippians 4:4; Colossians 3:15–17; 1 Thessalonians 5:16–18
[5] Hebrews 13:15   [6] Psalm 48:1

9 No turning back

In a solemn warning to those who said to Jesus 'I will follow you, Lord; but ...', Jesus replied, 'No one who puts his hand to the plough and looks back is fit for the kingdom of God.'[1] Although 95% of the verses which speak of our eternal place in God's kingdom give us the deep assurance that 'once a Christian, always a Christian' ('they shall *never* perish', *etc.*)— there is a 5% which warns us that we must not be glib or presumptuous in our relationship with God. It is extremely important, therefore, to go on with Christ once we have committed our lives to him. We are to 'endure to the end',[2] to 'be faithful unto death',[3] and to 'confirm our call and election'.[4] A surprising number of verses warn us against a superficial assurance.

It is wise, therefore, to settle it in your mind and heart that, with the help of Christ and the power of the indwelling Spirit, you will make it your own aim to please him. Christ calls us to a single-minded disciple-

[1] Luke 9:62
[2] Matthew 24:13
[3] Revelation 2:10; *cf.* 3:5
[4] 2 Peter 1:10

ship. Christians who are double-minded about this have the worst, not the best, of both worlds. They have too much of the world to enjoy Christ, and too much of Christ to enjoy the world. We never experience the incredible joy of Christ until we are wholly his. Even after years of dedicated service and rich spiritual experience Paul summed up his consuming ambition in five words: *'that I may know him'*.[5] Make this your supreme aim in life, and Christ will never, never disappoint you.

It is also of considerable importance to realize that every Christian is, strictly speaking, a missionary. 'As the Father has sent me,' said Jesus, 'even so I send you.'[6] Constantly he was sending his disciples into towns and villages, telling them to preach the good news of the kingdom of God. The church has often made the mistake of thinking and speaking of missionaries in the traditional terms of the past: some special Christians with unusual dedication doing daring pioneer work in exceptionally dangerous surroundings. The implication of all this is that such a calling is not for the ordinary Christian.

God, however, is a missionary God, who has sent his Son into this world. And God's work is missionary work. If we belong to God at all, we are already missionaries, in the best sense of that word. It is simply up to the Lord of the harvest to decide which part of the harvest fields of his world you and I are to work in. The needs everywhere are vast. 42% of Africans are Muslim; 25% belong to tribal religions. Only 5% of those living in Asia (containing more than one half of the world's population) are Christians; yet only

[5] Philippians 3:10   [6] John 20:21

5% of today's Protestant missionaries are working in this vast field. Even in the West, with all its enormous Christian privileges, hundreds of millions have virtually no knowledge at all of the true gospel of Christ. Wherever you live and work, therefore, and whatever you are doing with your life, remember that first and foremost you are a missionary of Jesus Christ. Don't dream of what you might be doing one day for him. 'As now, so then' is a good Christian motto. It is only as we concentrate on living and speaking for Christ now, amongst our particular circle of friends and acquaintances, that we shall be useful to him later on. God's time is always now.

To enable us to be effective witnesses Christ promised his disciples the power of the Holy Spirit.[7] Although every Christian has the Spirit living within him,[8] not every Christian is filled with the Spirit;[9] and therefore the potential which we have in Christ[1] is not always fully realized. Nothing is more crucial for a Christian than to be filled, and to go on and on being filled, with the Holy Spirit. Only in this way can we know the love and life and power of Christ in our lives.

If we realize our need for the power of the Spirit, the teaching of Jesus in Luke 11 may be of special help to us.[2] Jesus told his disciples a delightfully human story of a man who had an unexpected visitor late at night. The traveller was hungry but the host's larder bare. So, although it was midnight, the host went round to a friend and started banging at the

[7] Acts 1:8
[9] Ephesians 5:18
[2] Luke 11:5–13

[8] Romans 8:9
[1] Ephesians 1:3

door: 'A friend of mine has arrived on a journey, and I have nothing to set before him—lend me three loaves!' The man, woken suddenly from his sleep by this dreadful banging, was not exactly enthusiastic. But so persistent was his friend that eventually he got up and gave him whatever he needed.

What a vivid picture! There are people all around us with immense needs, and so often we feel that we have 'nothing to set before' them. Our spiritual larder is bare. The point of the parable, of course, is that if a grumpy old man at midnight will give his friend 'whatever he needs ... how much more will the heavenly Father give the Holy Spirit to those who ask him!'

Jesus anticipated, however, two common problems for the Christian who wants the power of the Spirit in his life. The first is *unbelief*: we may find it hard to believe that it can really happen. One day, perhaps, but not now. But the full power of the Spirit is part of our rich inheritance in Christ. To encourage our faith, therefore, Jesus underlines his promise six times: 'Ask, and it will be given you; seek, and you will find; knock, and it will be opened to you. For every one who asks receives, and he who seeks finds, and to him who knocks it will be opened.' In other words, it will happen, if you only believe.

The second problem is *fear*. What will God do with our lives? What are we letting ourselves in for? Again Jesus reassures us: 'What father among you, if his son asks for a fish, will instead of a fish give him a serpent?' Now, if we give good gifts to our children, evil though we be, 'how much more will the heavenly Father give the Holy Spirit to those who ask him!'

Naturally, we must first of all be in a right relationship with God, having repented of all known sin, and being willing to obey him. But providing those conditions are fulfilled, we must come and ask for the Holy Spirit to fill our lives. Don't worry about experiences. They will vary from person to person. Remember that Jesus meant exactly what he said. He also told us to believe that we *have* received, whenever we pray, and then God will surely give us what he has promised in order that he might be more glorified in our lives.

There is no limit to what God can do through anyone who is fully surrendered to his Son, filled with his Spirit, and an active member of the body of Christ, sharing and working with others according to the will of God. Indeed anything less than that is to slight the incredible mercy of God towards us. Paul, having summed up in the first eleven chapters of Romans the astonishing riches of God's love in setting us free from the guilt and power of sin and from the misery of death, comes to his conclusion: 'With eyes wide open to the mercies of God, I beg you, my brothers, as an act of intelligent worship, to give him your bodies, as a living sacrifice, consecrated to him and acceptable by him. Don't let the world around you squeeze you into its own mould, but let God remould your minds from within, so that you may prove in practice that the plan of God for you is good.'[3]

The only right and worthy response to God's mercy is *practical*, involving our bodies and minds; it is *total*, as we hold nothing back and offer ourselves as a 'living sacrifice'; and it is *purposeful*: instead of being pas-

[3] Romans 12:1, 2 (J. B. Phillips)

sively squeezed into the shapes and standards of the world, we deliberately give our bodies to God, and so let him work within our minds by his Spirit and his Word, that we increasingly think his thoughts and walk in his ways.

Of course it is not easy. Paul goes on in Romans 12 to explain that it includes using every God-given gift in Christ's service and for the sake of others. It means genuine love, pure lives, hard work, being aglow with the Spirit, patient prayer, generous giving and warm hospitality. It involves a spirit of forgiveness, harmonious relationships and a determined effort to be a peacemaker, however costly it may be to our pride. No, it is not easy. But neither was it easy for Jesus to come to this world, to be despised, and rejected, beaten, spat upon, deserted, falsely accused, and finally strung up on the most horrific instrument of torture and shame known to the ancient world.

A young man was walking round an art gallery, without any thought of Christ or Christian service. As he paused to look at Stenburg's painting of the crucifixion, the agony of that scene began to grip his imagination, and he noticed these words underneath the picture: 'All this I did for thee. What hast thou done for me?' He stood there motionless until the love and mercy of God in Jesus Christ urged him to present his whole life to God without reservation. From that brief moment in the art gallery a great missionary movement was born, resulting in countless men and women finding new life and freedom in Christ.

God has given you a fresh start in your life: a new birth, a new set of relationships, new attitudes, new values and a new purpose. Where you go from here, to a large extent, depends on you. What next? With eyes wide open to God's mercy I beg you, as an act of intelligent worship, to give him your body, and all that you have, as a living sacrifice, totally surrendered to Jesus Christ and filled with his Spirit. Make this your supreme aim in life from now onwards, and your life, and the lives of others through you, will be immeasurably enriched.

Further reading

Basic Christian faith

Michael Green, *Runaway World* (IVP). Who are the escapists of today? Not Christians, but those who refuse to face the facts, especially of Jesus Christ.

Michael Green, *Man Alive!* (IVP). A lively examination of a foundation belief of the Christian faith: that Jesus rose from the dead and is alive today.

Michael Green, *Jesus Spells Freedom* (IVP). Jesus can answer man's desire to be free with the greatest freedom he can ever find.

John Stott, *Basic Christianity* (IVP). A clear statement of the basic truths of Christ and of the Christian faith.

David Watson, *My God is Real* (Falcon). For those wanting to know the reality of God in their personal lives.

David Watson, *In Search of God* (Falcon). A guide through the confusion and doubts of today to a personal relationship with the living God.

John Young, *The Case against Christ* (Falcon). A positive look at some of the commonest objections to the Christian faith.

Christian living

Michael Green, *New Life, New Lifestyle* (Hodder and Stoughton). An excellent practical guide to full Christian living for those who have recently started.

Michael Griffiths, *Consistent Christianity* (IVP). How Christianity should work out on the practical level of attitudes and relationships.

Michael Griffiths, *Cinderella with Amnesia* (IVP). An exciting book about what God's new community—the church—is meant to be.

Paul Little, *How to Give Away your Faith* (IVP). A cartoon-illustrated guide to help Christians share their faith with other people.

Anne Townsend, *Prayer without Pretending* (Scripture Union). An honest book dealing with the doubts and value of praying for others.

David Watson, *One in the Spirit* (Hodder and Stoughton). An explanation of the person and work of the Holy Spirit.

Christian biography

Roland Bainton, *Here I Stand* (Mentor). An inspiring biography of one of history's greatest Christians, Martin Luther.

David Bentley-Taylor, *My Love Must Wait* (IVP). The story of Henry Martyn, who sacrificed everything—even the girl he loved—to serve his Lord.

Corrie ten Boom, *The Hiding Place* (Hodder and Stoughton). A runaway bestseller, speaking of the triumph of God's love under Nazi domination and in concentration camps.

Brother Andrew, *God's Smuggler* (Hodder and Stoughton). A thrilling bestseller about taking Bibles into communist countries, showing that God is at work in dangerous situations.

Keith Miller, *The Taste of New Wine* (Word). A very honest book in which the author shares his experience of learning to live and communicate with other Christians.

Helen Morgan, *What Price Glory?* (IVP). The absorbing story of a missionary, showing what missionary work is all about.

Helen Roseveare, *Give Me This Mountain* (IVP). A moving record of God's faithfulness in the midst of Congo violence. Fresh, honest, and very human.

Richard Wurmbrand, *In God's Underground* (Hodder and Stoughton). A prisoner in communist hands, beaten, starved and put in solitary confinement, Wurmbrand shows the sufficiency of God in times of severe suffering.

Bible study

Clive Charlton (editor), *Learning to Live* (IVP). A programme of daily Bible readings lasting six months, with questions to help you draw out the meaning and relevance of each passage.

Alan Stibbs (editor), *Search the Scriptures* (IVP). The method of study is the same as that of *Learning to*

Live, but the course is more advanced and covers the whole Bible in three years.

John Stott, *Understanding the Bible* (Scripture Union). This book gives practical help on the relevance, purpose, trustworthiness and over-all message of the Bible.

Scripture Union notes. Various types of reading-programmes and notes are available. For full details write to the Bible Reading Department, Scripture Union, 47 Marylebone Lane, London W1M 6AX.